Original title:
The Tropics Within Reach

Copyright © 2025 Creative Arts Management OÜ
All rights reserved.

Author: Aidan Marlowe
ISBN HARDBACK: 978-1-80581-536-5
ISBN PAPERBACK: 978-1-80581-063-6
ISBN EBOOK: 978-1-80581-536-5

Serenade by the Sea

Seagulls serenade with a squawk,
While crabs do a jig on the rock.
The waves groove in a salty beat,
Shells dance along, oh what a treat!

With each splash, a silly sound,
A fish wears a hat, oh what a clown!
The sun waves hello, as if to say,
Join the party, come out and play!

Parrots in Flight

Parrots wear shades, on a sunny spree,
Swinging on branches, they laugh with glee.
One claims to surf, another skates,
Who knew birds could have such great fates?

In a riot of colors, they chatter and squawk,
Trading their secrets as they mock.
Every tree is a stage for their show,
The jungle's own stars, putting on a glow!

Anemones and Evening Stars

Anemones wiggle with giddy delight,
As stars peek out, shining so bright.
The ocean hums a tuneful tune,
While jellyfish float like balloons in June.

Crabs throw a rave in the silver foam,
Dancing like kings in their gooey home.
The night is a canvas, laughter splays,
Painting memories in the waves' gentle plays.

Maracas and Mangoes

Maracas shake with a funky flair,
Mangoes rolling without a care.
Tropical beats fill the air with cheer,
Even the pineapples start to steer!

Giggling lizards join in the fun,
Playing tag under the bright sun.
With every twirl, they lose their hats,
Who knew nature was so full of spats?

The Dance of Fragrant Petals

In a garden of laughter, petals sway,
Dancing with bees in a sunny ballet.
The roses gossip, the tulips cheer,
While daisies sneak sips of the buzzing beer.

A parrot in shades, oh what a sight,
Tells jokes to the sun, shines warm and bright.
With cada step, a fragrant delight,
Even the cacti join in the light.

Sunset Serenade

A mango-shaped sun drips sweet on the bay,
As crabs on the shoreline waddle and play.
The waves form a chorus, a splashy refrain,
While seagulls dive down, in quest for their grain.

The beach ball bounces, so full of glee,
But waits for the wave like a clumsy puppy.
As shadows stretch long, we throw in our bets,
On who'll be the last to get their sun sets.

Journey to Solitude's Harbor

Off we sail on a banana boat,
As the clouds poke fun at our sunburnt coat.
With each splash and giggle, the sea takes its toll,
And jellyfish tease us, all jiggly and full.

We anchor in laughter, under the palm,
As coconuts drop, with a fruity charm.
A crab steals our snacks, with a cheeky flip,
While we sip on our coconuts, making a trip.

Cradled in Warmth

Wrapped in a towel like a burrito,
I dream of the ocean, and shout, "Let's go!"
But the sofa just chuckles, my warmth it knows,
While the ceiling fans twirl like it's all a show.

The remote spins tales of voyages grand,
As I munch popcorn with my lazy hand.
Comfy and cozy, I drift and I sway,
In my living room haven, I'll dance all day.

Whispers from the Coral Shore

The clams all gossip, they gossip loud,
While seagulls strut, acting rather proud.
A crab moonwalks, sideways he goes,
While parrots chuckle at the funny shows.

Sandcastles topple with a gentle breeze,
As I sip my drink beneath swaying trees.
Mermaids giggle, flipping their tails,
While dolphins surf, leaving silly trails.

Harvesting the Light of Dreams.

Bright coconuts drop with a thud and a twist,
The sun gives a wink, it can't be missed.
I chase after shadows in a flip-flop race,
While iguanas lounge with a chill in their grace.

Tiki torches flare with a flicker and dance,
As fireflies blink, we join in a prance.
Laughter erupts like a wave in the night,
We gather 'round flickers, all feeling just right.

Island Whispers

Turtles debate whether to swim or nap,
While my hat sails off in a funny mishap.
Palm fronds flutter, sharing secrets so bright,
As I giggle along with the stars in the night.

Bananas hang low, like they're eager to drop,
The island's a circus, it's hard to stop.
With piña coladas and laughter in air,
Every moment a jest, a joy to share.

Palms in the Breeze

The breeze tickles noses, a whimsical tease,
As palm trees shimmy, doing the kazoo with ease.
Shells barter tales with the waves as they roll,
While crabs form a band, oh what a nice stroll!

Sunburned tourists sprawl on the sand,
Trying to hold on, what a funny stand!
With skin like lobsters and laughter so loud,
We embrace the chaos, so silly and proud.

Ocean's Embrace

The waves giggle and laugh, oh what a sight,
Seagulls squawk in joy, taking flight.
Flip-flops forgotten, on sandy shores,
What's that? A crab? It's knocking at doors.

Coconuts drop with a plop in the sun,
Did that bird just steal my snack? What fun!
Beach towels spread out like a giant quilt,
Catching rays while we flirt with the guilt.

The ocean whispers jokes, they tickle my ear,
With each splash, the silliness draws near.
A sunburned nose, a silly surprise,
Here's to laughter beneath those blue skies.

As the tide rolls in, I leave my woes,
Laughter abounds as the ocean flows.
Caught in the splash of a playful spree,
Who knew the sea would be so funny?

Sun-Kissed Dreams

Under a sun that's a bit too bold,
I dance with a shadow, oh so uncontrolled.
Sunglasses on, like a superstar,
Tripping over flip-flops—look at me go far!

Ice cream cones that drip in the heat,
I giggle as it melts, my sticky sweet treat.
Sand castles rise while my hat flies away,
A quick chase ensues, oh, what a display!

Bright laughter echoes, like notes in the air,
We juggle beach balls, showing off flair.
With each goofy fall, I snort out a cheer,
Who knew such fun would lead to a smear?

The sun's setting slow, with a wink of delight,
We dance in the rays, oh, what a sight!
With sand on my nose, and joy in my chest,
In this sunny circus, I feel so blessed!

Verdant Horizons

In jungles where the monkeys play tricks,
I trip on vines; they giggle, what a fix!
Leafy hats? Oh yes, my new fashion trend,
Swaying with palms, I'm the jungle's best friend.

Parrots squawk style tips, "Be bold, be bright!"
Trying to blend, I'm a whimsical sight.
A lizard peeks out, offers a wink,
Did it just suggest we should go grab a drink?

Fragrant flowers tease my nose with their cheer,
As I tumble and stumble with fa-la-la fear.
The trees lean in close, whisper secrets anew,
I laugh at their tales, oh what else could ensue?

With a flourish and flair, I leap in delight,
The jungle is merry, morning till night.
Such antics abound, where the wild things can roam,
In this leafy kingdom, I've found my true home!

Lush Desires

A hammock swings low, casting shadows of dreams,
While sipping on smoothies, life's sweeter than seems.
Banana peels slip, I fumble and tumble,
Oh look, a fruit bowl—now that's a rumble!

A coconut shell hat makes me feel quite dapper,
I waddle around like a charming old flapper.
With fruits like confetti, I feast with a grin,
Grapefruit for hats, now that's how to win!

The scent of fresh guava fills up the air,
I dance with my smoothie, oh don't you dare stare!
Grass skirts and laughter, a grown-up affair,
The world's a big playground; let's all be aware!

As twilight descends, I twirl with delight,
In this lively land, everything feels right.
With buddies and giggles, oh what a spree,
In lushness and joy, we keep it carefree!

Aloha at Dusk

A surfboard's my trusty steed,
It rides the waves with quite the speed.
Flip-flops flying, as I dash,
I trip on sand—but what a splash!

A coconut drinks with a tiny straw,
Sipping slowly, oh what a flaw!
Seagulls squawk, demanding a bite,
As I laugh—what a comical sight!

The sunset paints skies in bold tints,
While I mix up my dance with chintz.
Hula moves gone a bit awry,
I just wink and say, 'Oh my!'

So here's to laughter, to sand-stuck toes,
To mishaps nobody really knows.
Life on the coast is a goofy ride,
With beach vibes that just can't hide!

Paper Lanterns Above

Balloons float high, take a look!
They wobble about like a storybook.
Each stringy dance, a giggly show,
As I pretend that I might glow!

Paper lanterns swing on a breeze,
Chasing sparrows with all their ease.
One tangled up in my wild hair,
I chuckle; who knew it'd want to share?

The night comes alive, the snacks in hand,
Lime soda spills in the warm sand.
I toast to stars that twinkle so bright,
But I'm more amazed by my soda fight!

So come one, come all to this funny fest,
Where lanterns and laughter are surely the best.
With silly mishaps and tasty treats,
We gather 'round for rhythmic beats!

Fireflies in the Dark

Dance of the bugs, with flicks of light,
Fireflies zooming, oh what a sight.
I try to catch one in my palm,
But it wiggles away—how alarming!

With a jar in hand, I make my plea,
To trap a spark and set it free.
Yet they giggle, dart left and right,
Seems they've turned this into a fight!

A family picnic turned into a race,
While I chase bugs in a clumsy place.
The flashlight's lost, oh what a guess,
I stumble, then trip, in my cute summer dress!

So here's to the chaos of buzzing friends,
Who light up the night until it ends.
Well, I may not have caught one spark,
But laughter lights up the dark!

Vibrant Oasis

Under palms, I sip my drink,
With a twist of lime, I smile and wink.
The floaty in the pool, a beastly sight,
I bob like bacon, what a delight!

Sunburned toes, they curl in glee,
As kids splash around, all carefree.
A wild swim race, chaos all around,
Am I the dolphin, or did I drown?

Parrots squawking, a lively tune,
I've got my shades, but not a clue.
They might judge me—a little fright,
When I dance like jelly under the light!

So here's to summers so vibrant and bright,
Filled with giggles and silly fright.
In this quirky slice of a sun-soaked day,
We laugh out loud—come what may!

Sunlight's Caress

Sunshine peeked through the leaves,
Like a child playing tricks,
Whispers of warm, giggling breeze,
Kisses me, oh so quick.

Lizards sunbathe on my toes,
With a pompous little pose,
They think they own this golden space,
In their vibrant, scaly clothes.

Coconuts roll—they tumble down,
Bouncing off my sunburned crown,
As if they're in a race, you see,
Laughing at my silly frown.

Sunglasses sit atop my nose,
Doing the tango as it goes,
While I sip my fruity drink,
And ponder if it's wine or prose.

Secrets of the Rainforest

In the jungle, mischief thrives,
Monkeys plotting fun-filled dives,
Swinging from the branches high,
Their laughter, a joyful vibe.

Parrots squawk with colorful flair,
Gossiping without a care,
Spilling secrets of the night,
With a wink, they take to air.

A sloth took five naps today,
Said he'd nap the time away,
While I chase the fireflies,
He just smiles and starts to sway.

Tropical plants throw a grand ball,
Dressed up, oh quite a sprawl,
They sway while the critters dance,
In a nature-fueled free-for-all.

Waves of Serenity

Waves crash down with a flip and splash,
Sending glimpses of life in a flash,
The crabs throw a party on the shore,
Dancing without a hint of bash.

Surfboards, like bright bananas, glide,
With riders who never seem to hide,
They wipe out, but with laughter loud,
Emerging wet, taking it in stride.

Seagulls compete in a lofty race,
Diving for snacks, oh what a chase,
I'm dodging their aerial tricks,
As chips fly past my silly face.

Beach umbrellas become giant hats,
Providing shade for playful chats,
Underneath them, tales unfold,
Of mischief shared with all our spats.

Exotic Melodies

Drums beat softly in the night,
Echoes dance with pure delight,
While hula skirts sway like sea,
In a rhythm, oh so bright.

Coconuts join in the fun,
With a smile for everyone,
Dancers leap and twirl about,
Till the stars blush one by one.

Flip-flops tap along the beat,
With laughter that can't be beat,
The shadows moving like they know,
How to make the night complete.

A ukulele strums a tune,
By the silver light of the moon,
As crickets sing their little hearts,
Celebrating under the boon.

Celestial Shores

Sandy toes in flip-flops, what a sight,
Seagulls squawking, giving me a fright.
Ice cream drips down my wrist, oh dear,
I'll definitely need a towel here!

Sunburned nose, a scoop of joy,
The beach ball bounces like a happy toy.
I wear sunglasses despite the haze,
Trying to impress with my silly ways.

A crab scuttles by in quite a dash,
I leap up quick—oh, what a splash!
My lemonade's wobbly, it tips and spills,
Who knew fun could bring such thrills?

The sunset paints the sky so bright,
Got sand in my hair, what a funny sight!
With each laugh, I feel so free,
In this paradise of lunacy.

Tropical Reverie

Beneath the palm trees, I sit and dream,
A coconut's my funniest regime.
Sipping juice from a straw, what a show,
It's slippery fun, just like a slip-n-slide, whoa!

The fruits are dancing, what a charade,
Bananas in hats, oh the fun they made.
Mangoes gossiping, spilling all the tea,
Their juicy secrets shared with glee!

Chickens strut with an air of pride,
Waddling around, they're full of stride.
I chase my sombrero, flying in haste,
But I can't stop laughing—this is pure taste!

Even the lizards join in the jest,
Living their best lives, a true fest.
In this realm where silliness thrives,
I feel more alive than I have in my drives.

Swaying Canopies

In the shade of leaves, I sway side to side,
As monkeys swing past, filled with pride.
With a grin on their face, they toss a few nuts,
I'm dodging their gifts, oh man, what a ruts!

Sunbeams peek through the leafy parts,
Like nature's confetti, it plays with hearts.
The breeze tells jokes, I can hardly keep,
As I giggle at squirrels that leap like sheep!

Palm fronds rustle, whispering secrets sweet,
While geckos do dances—what a treat!
Lost in a dance that's wonderfully absurd,
These lively moments can scarce be heard.

A parrot squawks its outrageous quip,
Nearby, a sloth takes a long, slow trip.
Here in this jungle, laughter's our guide,
Amongst quirky friends, I take a ride.

Mango-Scented Days

Under the sun, I find my bliss,
Mango slices taste just like a kiss.
Laughing with friends, we chase after flies,
Sporting our shades, we look like wise guys!

The ice cream truck's got its horn in tune,
Racing to catch it under the noon.
A cone in each hand, we parade along,
Singing hot tunes to the seagull's song.

With splashes and giggles, we dive from the shore,
Watermelons bob, kids begging for more.
A beach ball bounces, a colorful flare,
Catching the joy, I toss without care.

As the stars sprinkle down, we gather 'round tight,
Telling tall tales filled with delight.
Mango-scented dreams drift through the night,
In this silly slice of paradise, life feels right.

Sunsets with a Kiss

The sun dips low, a fiery tease,
A cheeky wink from swaying trees.
With sangria dreams and laughter shared,
A sunset's blush, no worries spared.

Ice cream drips on beachy toes,
As evening whispers, the cool wind blows.
We race the tide, our shoes in hand,
Every splash feels like magic sand.

Seagulls squawk in silly flight,
Chasing shadows in fading light.
We stumble on in sandy shirts,
Making memories, and laughing girts.

Oh, what fun, with stars to guide,
In this haven, we take our ride.
With every kiss, the sun will blush,
And life, my friend, is all a rush.

Chasing Paradise

A parrot mocks with vibrant flair,
As we dance close without a care.
Flip-flops pop, a joyful sound,
In this place, pure joy is found.

The ice cream truck is rolling near,
Jokes are traded, laughter clear.
With each cone, the world stands still,
Sipping coconut, a sweet thrill.

We dodge the rain, a playful game,
As puddles leap to make us lame.
Yet in this fun, we splash and play,
Chasing smiles through the day.

Tomorrow waits with echoes bright,
In our hearts, the sun's last light.
And as we run, so wild and free,
This chase of joy was meant to be.

Lush Hues of Dawn

Awake with giggles, the sun is shy,
Paints the sky as the parrots fly.
With sleepy heads and morning cups,
We watch the sunlight fill our ups.

Pineapple twists in our fruity bowls,
Nature dances, it tugs at our souls.
Toasting to waves that tickle our toes,
With each sip, the laughter flows.

A monkey swings, a banana thief,
Bringing us joy and comic relief.
We giggle as he snatches our brunch,
It's the best way to start a hunch.

As hues of dawn lay soft and sweet,
Our charming chaos is hard to beat.
With every dawn, the fun grows bright,
In this wild, whimsical morning light.

Margaritas and Moonlight

Sipping lime on the patio,
Imaginary waves put on a show.
With silly straws and playful jests,
We toast to life and all its quests.

The moon's a spotlight, bright and bold,
As secrets whispered, stories told.
A lizard darts, a cheeky sprite,
Bringing giggles to our night.

Melodies from the ocean's call,
We dance soon after, hearts enthralled.
Our margaritas, all aglow,
In some twisted limbo, we steal the show.

As stars above twinkle and tease,
We stumble 'round, trying to please.
With every sip, the world feels right,
In margaritas and moonbeams bright.

Journeys to Hidden Sanctuaries

In search of places, bright and cheery,
Where the sun is hot, and legends are dreary.
With a map upside down, we take a wrong turn,
Finding a spot where the seaweed will burn.

Chasing coconuts that roll down the hill,
While dodging the crabs that seem to have will.
We stumbled upon a hammock, oh such a swing,
'Twas tied to a palm, the laughter it brings.

A parrot squawks jokes in the shade of a tree,
Where sunscreen and laughter mix perfectly.
We discover our snacks have been stolen, oh dear,
By a raccoon in shades, who's embracing the cheer.

With whispers of secrets on a warm salty breeze,
Laughter erupts, as we chill with such ease.
These hidden sanctuaries spark joy in our stride,
Where memories linger, we call it our pride.

Sparrows in Sundown

As the sun dips low with a fiery glow,
Sparrows gather round, putting on quite the show.
They chirp like old friends sharing tales of the day,
While one takes a bow, but forgets what to say.

A dance in the dusk, they leap and they flit,
One lands on my shoulder—hey, buddy, don't sit!
They're gossiping loud on a branch up above,
About the one sparrow who found him a love.

With beaks full of berries, they laugh in delight,
While trying to balance, oh what a sight!
Unruly and fearless, they flap their own wings,
As the sunset fades, it's their song that springs.

These sparrows remind us as daylight does fade,
That laughter's the sound we should never evade.
With each sunny sundown, let our spirits lift high,
In the best kind of company, let laughter apply.

Luaus and Laughter

At a party with flowers, and grass skirts abound,
We feast on some fish, and the jokes fly around.
The hula is shaky, our moves out of sync,
But who cares when the punch bowl is filled to the brink?

Uncle Lou in the corner attempts to do flips,
While Auntie's just trying to keep her chips.
The ukulele strums a tune that's so sweet,
As Grandma spills sauce all over her feet.

There's dancing in circles, a clumsy parade,
As someone attempts to throw shade in the shade.
With laughter contagious, we all join the fun,
Shimmies and giggles beneath setting sun.

These luaus we cherish, with joy they do bring,
A blend of mishaps in which we can sing.
With friends gathered 'round and our hearts feeling bright,
Let's make every moment a laugh-filled delight.

Surfboard Dreams

With a surfboard tucked under my arm, I arise,
Dreaming of waves even dolphins would size.
I dash to the beach, bikini all set,
But the ocean's on lunch; it's a low tide threat.

I wobble and tumble, my balance a game,
While the seagulls all stare, looking proud, not the same.
A wave finally comes, and I'm ready to soar,
But end up just splashing—what a watery score!

My friends on the shore can't help but just snicker,
With cameras in hand, oh, how they do flicker.
A wipeout or two, but I'm back on my feet,
Just a fish out of water, feeling the beat.

But dreaming of surfing is fun in the sun,
With laughter and joy, how we all come undone.
Who cares if I wipe out or just take the plunge?
With surfboard dreams, we all laugh and we lunge.

Treasures of the Heart's Harbor

In a cove made of giggles, we sail,
Where bananas wear hats and tell a tall tale.
The parrots are gossiping, quite out of hand,
While sunbeams are discoing on glittering sand.

Nuts roll like marbles, a funny parade,
As jellybeans bounce in the sweet lemonade.
The coconuts chuckle with all of their might,
Hiding secrets that bring giggles at night.

Laughter floats on the waves, oh so fine,
With jellyfish dancing in a conga line.
We whisper to seashells, they wink and they nod,
The treasures we find are just whims of the odd.

In the harbor of hearts, joy's sails always billow,
With playful winds that tickle and chortle.
Come join the fun, there's a punch and a quip,
In a world where joy's always ready to flip!

Enchanted Echoes of Dusk

As the sun melts like butter on a warm piece of bread,
The stars start their chatter, soft words in our head.
Crickets hold concerts, so lively and clear,
While fireflies dance, bringing romance and cheer.

The dreams are like piñatas, so colorful and bright,
Filled with giggles and tickles and stardust delight.
With every sweet echo, we snicker and thrive,
In the twilight's warm clamour, we come all alive.

Clouds wear funny hats, just as night starts to fall,
We giggle at shadows that bounce on the wall.
The moon gives a wink, with its mischievous grin,
In a world of the quirky, where fun's the best sin.

With magical whispers that twirl in the gloom,
Laughter escapes like a flower in bloom.
In this dusk of delight, we find joy in the sound,
Echoes of bliss in the night all around.

Lullabies of Lush Retreats

In a canopy world, where the leaves shimmer bright,
Lullabies flutter like butterflies in flight.
The mango trees chuckle, their branches so wide,
As the cocoa beans giggle, and gather with pride.

Beneath the green arches, life sways to the beat,
With frogs in bow ties, tapping time with their feet.
While squirrels tell stories to clouds fluffy white,
It's a party of pleasures from morning to night.

In the heart of the jungle, where laughter's a stream,
We toast to the dreams that twinkle and gleam.
A rumble of giggles, a chorus of fun,
As the sun takes its bow, saying, "Wasn't that fun?"

So come take a nap on a bed made of leaves,
And wake to the sounds that the jungle conceives.
In lush retreats, where the joy's at its peak,
We dance with the whimsy, giggling and sleek.

Dance of the Daring Winds

Oh, the winds twist and twirl like a dervish in play,
With stories and giggles to brighten the day.
They whirl through the flowers, tickling their toes,
Carrying whispers of mischief, who knows?

The palm fronds all wiggle, a hilarious sight,
And the breezes invent games, from morning to night.
With a chuckle, the zephyrs sneak up on the sand,
Bringing bursts of pure laughter, just as they planned.

A banana boat sails on dreams full of zest,
While gales spread their laughter, no time to rest.
The playful gusts challenge the birds in the sky,
As they swoop and they soar, oh how they fly high!

So ride on the winds, let your worries be free,
In a dance of pure joy, come and twirl with me.
For when laughter is carried on the fluffs of the breeze,
We find ourselves dancing with the utmost ease.

Rhythms of the Land

In a hammock strung too tight,
I swung and lost my fight.
The mango fell from high above,
And splattered me with sticky love.

Parrots screech in loud delight,
As I dance like a clumsy kite.
With every beat my feet do blow,
I'd stand still, but who wants slow?

Coconuts roll by surprise,
They race me with their nutty eyes.
My sunburnt nose is quite the sight,
I laugh till day turns into night.

Bees buzz like they've found a beat,
While I attempt to make my feet.
The rhythm makes the world all shake,
And that's how great adventures wake.

A Tapestry of Leaves

In the jungle, I saw a tree,
With leaves that whispered secrets to me.
A parrot joked, 'Try climbing high!'
But as I slipped, I let out a sigh.

Lianas tangled in my hair,
As monkeys laughed with playful flair.
One stole my hat; what a sly chap,
Chased by the sounds of goofy clap!

Bamboo sways like it's got some groove,
While I attempt my own cool move.
But the ground catches me by surprise,
As I roll with laughter, to my surprise!

Nature weaves with colors bright,
My sun-kissed soul takes flight tonight.
Each leaf a prankster, with glee they weave,
In this tapestry, I believe!

Veils of Ocean Mist

The ocean's laughter calls me near,
With salty jokes and waves of cheer.
I tried to swim, but oh what fun,
Instead I splashed—now, look, I'm done!

Seaweed tickled my funny bone,
As I fumbled for my floating throne.
The fishy sneers and dolphin's grace,
I'm the clown in this watery place!

Shells whisper tales of salty lore,
I dance with crabs on the sandy floor.
They pinch and scuttle with quick delight,
While I trip over, oh what a sight!

The lighthouse waves a cheeky hello,
As I stumble in the ebb and flow.
In misty veils of laughter and glee,
The ocean's prank was made for me!

Sapphire Waters

In a boat made of rubber, we drift and we sway,
Chasing the fish that just laugh and play.
Sunburned noses and hats made of straw,
A seagull steals snacks—what a ridiculous flaw!

The water's so blue, it's hard to believe,
That high in the sky, the clouds all deceive.
We splash like we're dolphins, or maybe like whales,
While our flip-flops flap with the wind in their sails.

In wild inflatable, we dodge all the waves,
Pretending we're pirates, find treasure in caves.
Laughs echo louder than the waves' silly roar,
As sunscreen drips down, making goo on the shore.

A crab gives a wink, as if in on the joke,
While we trip over snacks and lose our cool yoke.
Beneath the blue skies, the laughter's our guide,
In sapphire waters, where joy cannot hide.

Fragrant Escapes

With mangoes and chili, a feast on the breeze,
We tango with ants that crawl up our knees.
Bananas grow bonkers, they dance in the sun,
While a parrot imitates every word that we've spun.

Pickled delight in a jar on the shelf,
We taste it together, take time for ourselves.
Palm trees are swaying to songs we can't hear,
As we laugh at the sun with a cold drink in gear.

The scent of the flowers plays tricks on our mind,
As we claim we're explorers, of the daring kind!
With a map made of napkins, we wander away,
Into fragrant escapes, where the laughter can't sway.

But watch out for bees that buzz with a sting,
Trying to join in on this tropical fling.
We run and we giggle, dodging pollen with glee,
In a world of sweet scents, it's wild and carefree!

Twilight in Eden

As the sun tips its hat and dips low in the sky,
We dance with the shadows that flicker and fly.
Swatting at fireflies, we giggle with glee,
While our ice cream cones melt—what a sight to see!

The palm fronds are whispering secrets so sweet,
Of a luau planned just for our two pair of feet.
Tiki torches flicker, like stars, in their prime,
We waltz through the evening, consumed by the rhyme.

A coconut laughs from high in its perch,
While we make a wish at an imaginary church.
We paint all our dreams on the fabric of night,
With laughter like bubbles, sparkling and bright.

As cicadas sing tunes, we spin 'round with flair,
Twilight in Eden, with whimsy to spare.
With joy wrapped in colors, we cherish the view,
Decorated by stars, our friendship is true.

Songs of the Coconut Grove

In the shade of the palms, we strum on our tunes,
While monkeys join in, they dance like buffoons.
Coconuts rattle and giggle with cheer,
As we sing our own songs for all critters to hear.

The breeze carries laughter, a melody fine,
While a lizard's solo steals much of our shine.
Bananas applaud, they're ripe with delight,
As we sway and we hum in the warm starlit night.

We're all part of a choir, the oddest brigade,
With cucumbers jiving, in a vegetable parade.
Bright drums made of shells sound out our refrain,
As crabs join the chorus, entertaining the grain.

So let's raise our voices, tis' a tropical show,
In the grove where the dances of goofy things flow.
Songs of the coconut, we'll serenade free,
Where laughter's a treasure, that's always in spree.

The Song of Mist and Mango

In the breeze, the mango sways,
A dance of joy on sunny days.
The misty laugh of morning's light,
Tickles the leaves in pure delight.

A parrot squawks, a monkey grins,
Chasing shadows, where fun begins.
In every fruit, a secret treat,
Nature's mischief, oh so sweet!

Bees are buzzing, lost in glee,
While sloths pretend to climb a tree.
The day's adventure, come what may,
With laughter echoing, we play.

So raise a toast to the sun's warm rays,
To tropical antics and playful ways.
Let joy be found in every glance,
A whimsical, wild, unending dance.

Hidden Blossoms in the Boughs

In shady groves where secrets dwell,
A blossom peeks, it's quite a yell!
It whispers colors, bold and bright,
Painting the trees with pure delight.

The monkeys play a game of tag,
While birds in hats begin to wag.
A playful breeze, it sings along,
With nature's choir, we hum a song.

Coconuts drop, a drumming beat,
While lizards bust out funky feet.
In this realm of shenanigans,
The laughter rings like maracas' spins.

So find those blooms, like gems they glow,
In this escapade, let's steal the show!
A world of wonders, we will fetch,
With smiles wide, and hearts that stretch.

Reflections of Warmth and Wonder

Sun-kissed cheeks and sandy toes,
A beach ball bounces, and laughter flows.
The ocean winks with a playful tease,
As shells join in a joyful breeze.

A crab in shades, struts with flair,
While seagulls squabble in the air.
The sun's warm grin, a friendly show,
In this carefree land, our spirits grow.

With every splash, a giggle bursts,
The tide delivers our playful thirsts.
And as the sunset twirls its art,
We gather 'round, each with a heart.

So let us play, as the stars appear,
With tales and laughter, we hold dear.
A tapestry of joy we weave,
In this canvas, all believe.

A Glimpse of Paradise

Underneath a palm's gentle sway,
Life's a carnival, come what may.
With hues of fruit and laughter bright,
Every moment feels just right.

A toucan dons its vibrant wear,
Sipping nectar, without a care.
While turtles groove, so slow and grand,
They dance along the golden sand.

Flip-flops flung in joyful flight,
Turn chores to games—all feels so light!
In this place where smiles unite,
Worries vanish, out of sight.

So let us cherish each silly jest,
In paradise, we find our zest.
With hearts alight, let laughter bloom,
As joy transforms each room.

Underneath a Swaying Sky

Underneath the bright blue sky,
There's a parrot with a tie.
It squawks around with such flair,
Mixing gossip in the air.

Flip-flops squeak on sandy trails,
As we chase the wind-filled sails.
Sunburned noses start to toast,
While the coconut drinks boast.

Dancing crabs show off their moves,
In a rhythm that grooves and grooves.
Watermelons roll so free,
As we giggle on the spree.

If the sun would just comply,
And not set so soon, oh my!
A sunset painted, oh so bright,
We'll dance until we lose the light.

Journey to Winding Shores

Off we go to winding shores,
Where the sand tickles our pores.
Crabs are crawling, looking sly,
While I try to catch the sky.

Mango juice drips from our chins,
As we laugh loud with silly grins.
The seagulls steal our tasty fries,
With their cunning, crafty eyes.

But then a wave does come crashing,
And all our dreams are splashing.
A flip, a flop, and oh dear me,
My sandwich lost to the sea!

Yet with each jolly, soaked hour,
We find joy in each fresh flower.
The beach beckons with laughter near,
An endless fun, a giant cheer!

Lush Dreams Awaken

In the garden where fruits sway,
I swear the grapes are here to play.
A coconut sings a tropical tune,
As I dance beneath the moon.

Sugarcane fields wipe my cares,
Giggling with ants as they share.
Bananas in hats, how absurd,
While pineapple bursts with a word!

Tropical breezes whisper light,
Bringing laughter and pure delight.
With every fruit, a funny tale,
In this haven where joys prevail.

Wake up, my friend, it's time to feast,
On laughter and fun, joy increased.
The lush dreams of this lively land,
Come alive by the sea and sand.

Beneath the Bounty of Stars

Beneath the sky, the stars delight,
We roast marshmallows through the night.
A firefly twirls, wears a crown,
While I try not to trip and drown.

The crickets play their funny tunes,
While we peek at the laughing moon.
A raccoon swipes our last s'more,
It's a party we can't ignore!

Tales of treasure float on the breeze,
With tales of pirates and their fees.
So we giggle and point at the trees,
Hoping to find a pirate's keys!

As dawn approaches, oh what a sight,
Dreams will dance, and spirits take flight.
Underneath these bright shining stars,
We'll keep laughing near and far.

Footprints in Warm Sand

With every step, my flip-flops flew,
I left a trail that looked like two.
Crabs waved claws, they thought it fun,
They danced around, under the sun.

Ice cream dripped right down my arm,
A seagull swooped; oh, such a charm!
My beach towel, oh what a mess,
I might just need a new sundress!

The sunbeams played hide and seek,
I swear I heard a coconut squeak.
My drink with a tiny umbrella,
Has become my own smack talk fella!

Happy laughter fills the air,
As I struggle with sand in my hair.
Footprints fade but joy remains,
In this sand, no one complains.

Senses Unfurled

A piña colada in one hand,
With coconut whispers, oh so grand.
I tried to dance in salsa style,
But tripped on my own carefree smile.

The mango's sweetness drips like gold,
A sticky treat, or so I'm told.
But ants think I'm a buffet feast,
I swat my hand and yell, "At least!"

The music sways, but so do I,
Is that a hammock or the sky?
With every sway, my snacks take flight,
Savory dreams in paradise light.

The sunset winks, it's time to play,
Lost in laughter, I must say hey!
This island life is such a tease,
Where joy comes easy, like a breeze.

In the Shade of a Banyan Tree

Beneath the branches, I take a seat,
My friend's loud snoring, quite a feat.
The leaves whisper tales, quite absurd,
Of lost flip-flops, not a word!

The monkeys swing and eye my snack,
I toss them chips, they never lack.
They chatter back, like they own the place,
I laugh aloud, can't help but face!

A squirrel drops down, quite the bold,
In search of treasures, or so I'm told.
I share my sandwich, just a bite,
It scurries off, oh what a sight!

The banyan tree is my good friend,
In its embrace, my worries end.
With giggles swirling in the air,
I find pure joy, without a care.

Cerulean Skies

The skies look painted, oh so bright,
With fluffy clouds that take to flight.
I squint and see a strange old shoe,
   Floating by, oh what a view!

Kites dance high with squeaky strings,
While laughter flutters, oh how it sings.
I trip on laughter, fall on grass,
   Chasing joy as fortunes pass.

Bubbles float, they shimmer and glide,
Like little dreams, they do not hide.
I reach to pop, but miss the chance,
And end up stuck in a silly dance.

As dusk arrives, the sky blushes red,
With twilight stories, my heart is fed.
In this kaleidoscope of cheer,
The world feels playful, close and near.

Ocean's Embrace

Waves giggle as they roll and sway,
Seagulls argue, they steal fish away.
Sunblock slathers in a comical spree,
A crab waves back, as happy as can be.

Beach balls bounce, they fly and crash,
A flip-flop lands with an awkward splash.
Sand castles crumble beneath the sun,
A king's crown lost; the beach is outdone.

The octopus dances in a funny way,
His tentacles twist, a bright ballet.
Splashing friends all shout in delight,
"Did you just see that? What a sight!"

As the tide pulls back with a playful cheer,
We laugh at the sea, our worries disappear.
Seashells sing, with a ticklish tune,
While we sip cocktails, under the moon.

A Soft Breeze at Dusk

The wind whispers secrets, just a tease,
Tickling my arm with the softest breeze.
A coconut falls, it's a true surprise,
"Hats off!" I yell, watching folks disguise.

Palm trees sway like they've lost their beat,
Shadows stretch out, dancing on bare feet.
Laughter erupts from a nearby pad,
Someone's barbecue smells truly rad.

Fireflies join in a light-hearted race,
Flickering laughter in the darkening space.
A gentle breeze carries jokes from afar,
About a crab who dreamed of being a star.

As the dusk settles, stars start to peek,
With nighttime stories that make us all squeak.
Days may end, but we rise with a grin,
For tomorrow, it starts all over again.

Dreaming of Mango Skies

Mango trees wave, wearing leafy hats,
While ants march by in tiny, silly spats.
Clouds fluff out like sweet cotton candy,
A delicious scene, a bit too dandy.

Pineapples giggle, tucked in their crowns,
As we dance around in our mismatched gowns.
The sun's a jester, playing peek-a-boo,
Turning the sky from bright gold to blue.

We splash in puddles, with carefree delight,
Seeking mangoes as our hearts take flight.
With every bite, laughter fills the air,
Sticky fingers, oh what a funny affair!

As day turns to night, the stars come alive,
We dream of mangoes, our laughter will thrive.
In this fruity world, no worries arise,
Just funny moments 'neath mango-filled skies.

Cascade of Colors

Colors tumble like a wacky parade,
Reds and yellows, all dressed to invade.
The sun dips low in a golden flare,
A rainbow of giggles in the warm air.

Painted skies inspire silly dreams,
As our laughter bubbles like playful streams.
A tie-dye sunset, winks at the night,
Who knew crayons could spark such delight?

Mismatched socks run wild on the beach,
While jellybeans giggle, just out of reach.
The evening unfolds in a colorful hug,
As we dive into fun, snug as a bug.

With the stars above, a glittering show,
We dance in breezes, letting cheer flow.
Every hue blends; we relish the cheer,
In this cascade of colors, we hold dear.

When Mangos Sing

The mangos dance in splendid glee,
They twirl and spin, oh can't you see?
A pit here, a pit there, what a mess!
But who can blame them for such zest?

Beneath a tree, they start to croon,
Sipping sunshine, a sweet monsoon.
If I could join, I'd wear a crown,
Made of green leaves, not upside down!

A parrot squawks, he wants to join,
"Come on, fellas, let's make some noise!"
While cats are hiding, looking stern,
"Why do they sing? When will they learn?"

As day turns dark, their voices fade,
Mangos dream in the twilight shade.
While folks with ice cream pass them by,
"Next time, don't leave us high and dry!"

Hibiscus Whispers

The flowers gossip in the breeze,
"Oh darling, did you see those bees?"
"No time for buzz, we're in full bloom,
Careful not to gather too much gloom!"

A ladybug stops for afternoon tea,
"Oh Hibiscus, what's the latest spree?"
She answers with a swirl and a sway,
"Just new guests here, an all-day ballet!"

Chasing butterflies, a wild delight,
"Floral fashion? That's quite the sight!"
While ants march in a strict parade,
"Oh for heaven's sake! Can't they invade?"

As sunlight wanes, the whispers grow,
A chuckle here and a giggle low.
When night falls, they'll dress up in stars,
"Best dressed flowers, let's raise the bars!"

Altitude of Amour

Two parrots perched on a coconut palm,
Exchanging sweet nothings with such calm.
"Do you love me, or just the view?
With skies so blue, it's hard to skew!"

A seagull swoops in, mid-fluff and flap,
"Lovebirds, stop! You're a real mishap!"
But they just giggle, unbothered and free,
"Fly on, dear gull, we're in harmony!"

The waves clap hands at the shore below,
"Love is a dance, come join the show!"
With every flap, the heart takes flight,
In a whirl of colors, a pure delight!

As clouds drift by, they'll share a toast,
"A toast to love, we adore the coast!"
With every sip of salty air,
"Altitude of amour, nothing can compare!"

Underneath the Starry Veil

Under the stars, a party unfolds,
Where laughter mingles with stories told.
Coconuts roll like playful little balls,
While crickets accompany with their calls.

A crazy crab joins the festive throng,
"Crack me open; you can't go wrong!"
While fireflies twinkle like tiny lights,
"The night's our stage; let's reach new heights!"

A dancing breeze pulls in all the fun,
As moonlit shadows dance, one by one.
The jokes take flight on the wings of night,
"Who knew the stars could shine so bright?"

With every cheer, the night grows bold,
A show of joy, never getting old.
Underneath the starry veil so high,
"Let's toast to dreams that flutter and fly!"

Echoes of Laughter in the Canopy

In a jungle, monkeys swing high,
Chasing shadows, they leap and fly.
With a banana, they hold their prize,
While parrots gossip with big, bright eyes.

Under tight vines, a tiger naps,
Dreaming of steak and heavenly laps.
But here comes an ant wearing a hat,
Now it's a party, imagine that!

The sun peeks through, a playful tease,
Bouncing mist and warm summer breeze.
Everyone's dancing, even a sloth,
Grooving softly at a snail's troth.

An iguana plays tunes on a leaf,
While the frogs croak out their belief.
In this wild place where joy's the key,
Every laugh echoes—come join the spree!

A Tapestry of Vivid Remembrance

A toucan flaunts its colors bright,
Waving hello with sheer delight.
Crickets chirp a rhythm grand,
This vibrant show, a merry band.

An old parrot tells tales quite tall,
Of a huge fish that wasn't small.
With every twist, we all lean in,
Waiting to cue the grand old grin.

The breeze carries laughter on its wings,
As all creatures join in on silly sings.
A turtle joins with a wiggly dance,
Who knew it had this quirky chance?

Together they weave a patchwork song,
Of memories shared and moments long.
Amidst the flora, their joy runs free,
In this whimsically woven jubilee.

Tropical Tides of Time

The waves crash down with a giggling sound,
While crabs do the cha-cha on the sand ground.
Coconuts roll, trying to escape,
As kids run by in an oversized cape.

A fish in a bowl gives a wise old wink,
While a beach ball dares the waves to sink.
Seagulls squawk like they run the place,
As sunbathers grin with a mischief face.

With a splash, surfboards ride the crest,
Riding high, guests wear their best.
Mermaids laugh off scandals past,
In this seaside circus, fun's unsurpassed.

Even the sun, with its golden rays,
Streaks through clouds on adventurous days.
Every tide pools out silly cheer,
Here laughter's a wave we hold so dear!

Woven with Rain and Sun

In the drizzle, a child spins fast,
Catching raindrops, a dance unsurpassed.
A pot-bellied pig snorts with glee,
Under the arch of a big leafy tree.

Sunshine breaks with a sparkling grin,
As puddles turn into a slide, let's begin!
Nearby, a goat leaps, with no care,
"Join me!" it bleats with a playfully flair.

A rainbow arches, bright and bold,
As young ones chase every spark untold.
In this garden of joy, nothing's too weird,
Even the flowers giggle, if you've heard!

Together they play, in the murky fun,
Each splash a beat, under rain and sun.
And as the day fades with a warm embrace,
The laughter lingers, in this wild place.

Butterfly's Dance

In a garden of color, they flit and they play,
With wings like confetti, brightening the day.
They dodge and they dart, in a whimsical chase,
Who knew tiny creatures could have such a pace?

They land on my nose, then they're off in a blink,
Is it me they adore, or the sweet nectar drink?
Their laughter is silent, but it's loud in my heart,
These butterflies know how to dance and depart.

They hold tiny parties on petals so sweet,
With a sip of the sunshine, they're dancing on feet.
I join in the fun, with a wiggle and spin,
But these nimble little things always win in the end!

So here's to the dance, the fluttering scene,
With friends made of velvet, and pockets of green.
Let's laugh with the butterflies, just like a kid,
In this garden of giggles, let's go, let's get mid!

Natural Symphony

A cacophony of chirps, a comedic delight,
The frogs play the rhythm, the crickets take flight.
While birds belt their anthems, so off-key yet bold,
It's nature's own concert, and it never gets old.

I thought I could join in, with a whistle or two,
But I scared a few critters, they fled like the dew.
A squirrel dropped his acorn, as I missed my cue,
Turns out I'm a solo in this nature's zoo!

Yet the laughter grows louder, as the beat carries on,
With each wacky note, my worries are gone.
The trees clap their branches, the flowers sway slow,
In a symphony wild, where all are aglow.

So come grab your maracas, and let's beat the ground,
In this crazy orchestra, joy's always around.
Forget all the rules, let your spirit take flight,
In this wacky natural show, the world feels just right!

Where the Wild Blooms

In a patch where the daisies giggle and grin,
For a crown made of flowers, who could dare sin?
The bees hold a rave, buzzing beats in the air,
While butterflies break dance without any care.

The sunflowers wave in their tall, golden gowns,
While the tulips insist it's time for more clowns.
The daisies declare: 'Let's have a parade!'
And I can't help but join in this floral charade.

Just watch out for thorns, they're humorless prudes,
While the roses gossip in their scented moods.
But laughter's the scent that wafts in the breeze,
In this garden of wild, where everyone's pleased.

So grab your green thumb and let's make some noise,
With petals as confetti, we'll revel in joys.
For in this wild bloom, we dance, sing, and play,
Life's a vibrant bouquet, let's celebrate each day!

Dreaming of Tropic Skies

There's a hammock of clouds, where the dreams like to swing,
Beneath blazing sun, that's the silliest thing.
The belly laughs come easy with breezes that tease,
As daydreams float by like a soft, swaying breeze.

The parrot's a jester, with colors so bright,
Imitating voices, he's a riot on flight.
With laughter so loud, he could wake up the sun,
I think he just won the 'Most Funny' award!

The waves tickle shores with their playful embrace,
While I try to dance, tripping over my grace.
But why should it matter, when the breeze blows just right,
And the heart of the day invites joy with its light?

In this dream world of whimsy, let's all take a chance,
To twirl with the palm trees and join in the dance.
So dream of the skies where the wild laughter flies,
In a place of pure joy, under tropical skies!

Dances with Coconuts

Under palm trees, fists are raised,
Coconuts dance, we're all amazed.
Hula skirts sway in the breeze,
Our laughter floats like honey bees.

Summer sun with a cheeky grin,
Tropical fruits make us spin.
Fruits that fall with a plop and thud,
We'll make a feast out of this dud.

Surfboards wobble, we take a dive,
Yeah, this place is truly alive!
Splashing water, we squeal and shout,
Coconuts rolling, there's no doubt!

Dance and twirl, the island calls,
With coconut hats, we'll dodge the falls.
All our worries we will toss,
In this paradise, we're the boss!

Woven Light

A hammock strung between two trees,
Catching rays with gentle ease.
Every glint, a wink from fate,
Here's a sunbeam, grab a plate!

Tropical drinks with umbrellas sway,
Do they need to be this gay?
Sipping smiles from a coconut shell,
Joking 'round, we laugh so well.

Light dances on a sandy floor,
Beneath our feet, the ocean's roar.
We weave our tales as the sun goes down,
In this bright paradise, we wear the crown.

Night falls soft like a friendly cat,
Counting stars, we can't find a mat.
But on this beach, who needs a bed?
We'll make do with laughter instead!

Chasing after Lushness

In a land where bananas grow,
We race the wind and steal the show.
With flip-flops flying, we take a leap,
Grassy fields that seem to creep.

Oh, the coconuts tease from above,
"Catch us if you can!" they shove.
We leap and duck, a fruit-filled dance,
Life's a game and we take a chance!

Chasing after that vibrant hue,
Everything's ripe, we can't misconstrue.
Colors burst like a joke so slick,
We're after laughter—quick, quick, quick!

Every sunset a painting bright,
We chuckle as day turns into night.
Chasing after joy, we have our fun,
Lushness found, and we've just begun!

Turquoise Horizons

Off we go where the sky meets sea,
A turquoise world calling me.
With sun hats on and shades so wide,
Joy's the compass, what a ride!

Seagulls prance, they laugh up high,
"Come and join, don't be shy!"
Barefoot dances on the sands so warm,
Lushness found in its vibrant charm.

Crabs sidestep, debate their fate,
Will they escape or simply wait?
While fish flicker in a turquoise spree,
Who knew colors could set us free?

With sunsets like a painting done,
This playful journey has just begun!
Laughing waves, let the world unfold,
Here in paradise, we'll be bold!

Silhouettes of Ylang-Ylang

In the garden, I prance like a bee,
Sniffing blooms, just me and my glee.
Ylang-ylang whispers sweet in my ear,
I wonder if flowers drink too much beer!

Butterflies dance, oh what a sight,
With fluttering wings, they take flight.
I joined their gala, what a big show,
But tripped on my toes, down I did go!

The leaves are my friends, they giggle and sway,
As I sing off-key, in my own way.
The sun's laughing bright, "You did great!"
Me and the blooms, we'll celebrate!

Swaying like palm trees, we finish this spree,
With flowers all around, forever carefree.
In this jungle, my spirit's set free,
Who needs a map, when you have just me?

Tropical Moonbeams

Under a sky, where the moon wears shades,
I dance with shadows, but oh, how it fades!
The glow in my drink, it looks like a star,
But it's just my umbrella from the bar!

Banana leaves rustle, join in my fun,
I swear they have gossip about everyone.
"Did you see that guy with too much cologne?"
They chuckle and whisper, in hushed undertone.

The waves gently laugh, tickling the shore,
While I ponder if mermaids love dance floors.
With a flip and a splish, I jump in the tide,
Making shells giggle as they try to hide.

Moonbeams are giggles from nighttime's fair hand,
And I twirl, I whirl, a one-person band.
With laughter and bubbles, my worries take flight,
In a dance with the waves, all feels just right!

Echoes of Distant Shores

From the shore, I hear whispers of sand,
Secrets of seashells, oh isn't it grand!
They tell tales of pirates, both bold and brave,
But I think they're just looking for a wave!

Crabs in their jackets are scurrying by,
With a pinch and a click, they seem to sigh.
"Not you again!" they grumble and pout,
I'm just trying to make some friends, no doubt!

The seagulls caw, as if they know me well,
They've seen my dance card, it's certainly swell.
"Can you step left?" one squawks with a smirk,
But I trip on my flip-flops, life's little quirk.

In the echoes of laughter, the breeze carries cheer,
The shores are alive, no room for a sneer.
With a wave and a shell, I'll take it all in,
As I dance with the tides, I'm sure to grin!

Coral Reefs and Seagrass

Beneath the waves where the fishes all play,
The corals are buzzing, what a bright ballet!
Sardines in formation, like a marching band,
While a sleepy old turtle strikes poses so grand!

Seagrass tickles, giving fish a ride,
They giggle and shimmer, full of pride.
"Catch me," they dart, like a game of tag,
But I just splash water, my moves a bit wag!

The octopus winks, then hides in his den,
Poking out slyly with three of his ten.
In this underwater circus, wild and free,
I blend in, hoping no one will see me!

Coral reefs chuckle in colors so bright,
As I float on by, in pure delight.
With treasures aplenty, my heart candid laughs,
At this sunshine kingdom of seagrass and chaffs!

Coral Mirage

In bright blue waters, fish do prance,
While I'm on land, trying to dance.
A crab scuttles by, it looks quite sly,
I think it winked—oh my, oh my!

The sun's a beacon, I'm feeling grand,
But I forgot sunscreen, oh isn't that bland?
Burnt like toast, I hobble and hop,
Next time I'll stay in, nope, never stop!

A parrot squawks, "Why wear that hat?"
It's big enough to fit a cat!
I smile at the bird, say, "You've got style,
But your fashion advice is quite vile!"

With fruity drinks, and sand so bright,
I'll laugh about this by the campfire light.
Life's comedy show, don't you see?
I'll take a tumble—but I'm still free!

Paradise Awaits

A piña colada in my hand,
Why's it so hard to find dry land?
I hop on a flamingo, it's quite a sight,
But it's just a pool float, oh what a fright!

The beach is calling, like a siren's song,
"Come soak in sun, it won't be long!"
But sand gets in places you can't believe,
I've lost a shoe; now I can't even weave!

Laughter erupts with each falling friend,
One slips on a shell—oh, what a trend!
We roll like seaweed, no better plan,
We're a goofy crew, the beach's biggest fan!

Take off those shoes, it's a fashion plight,
Barefoot adventures feel just right.
"Let's build a castle," we all decree,
But ours looks more like a pile of debris!

Heat-Haze Horizons

The sun is shining, a fiery glare,
But all I've got is one thin chair.
I try to tan, but alas I fry,
I look like a lobster, oh me, oh my!

Sweat beads trickle down my brow,
Oh, the heat is intense, I tell you now!
I wave to a squirrel, it rolls its eyes,
Even nature knows my sunburned lies!

Tropical drinks are stacked up high,
But my smoothie's now just a slushy pie.
I sip with joy, it's somewhat unreal,
But it's all gone, was that my last meal?

I chase the sunset, it's fading fast,
"Goodbye, hot day!"—it just blew past.
As evening settles, with fireflies in sight,
I'll dance with joy under the moonlight!

Hidden Valleys

In valleys lush where shadows play,
I trip on vines—oh what a display!
Nature's wit is cruel and sly,
I'm testing songs for a lost lullaby.

Bananas slip—not a great delight,
I tumble and roll; oh, what a sight!
The birds all laugh from branches above,
And I try to sing, but I scare off the dove.

I spot a stream, I take a dip,
But there's more moss than I'd like to grip.
Wobbling wild, I finally sigh,
"Life's a circus, and I'm the pie!"

Through hidden paths in groves so fine,
I lose my way, I'm not the divine.
Yet with every slip, each giggle and cheer,
I find adventure—it's perfectly clear!

www.ingramcontent.com/pod-product-compliance
Lightning Source LLC
Chambersburg PA
CBHW072121070526
44585CB00016B/1525